The Yale Center for British Art

The Yale Center for British Art

A Tribute to the Genius of Louis I. Kahn

text by Duncan Robinson

photographs by David Finn

Yale Center for British Art
Yale University Press
New Haven and London

Designed and set in Sabon type by Julie Lavorgna
Printed in Canada by Transcontinental

Library of Congress Cataloging-in-Publication Data
Robinson, Duncan.
The Yale Center for British Art : a tribute to the genius of Louis I. Kahn /
Duncan Robinson; with photographs by David Finn.
p.   cm.
Includes bibliographical references.
ISBN 0-300-06972-3 (pbk.)
ISBN 0-930606-82-5 (pbk.)
1. Yale Center for British Art.
2. Architecture, Modern — 20th century — Connecticut — New Haven.
3. Kahn, Louis I., 1901–1974 — Criticism and interpretation.
4. New Haven (Conn.) — Buildings, structures, etc. I. Kahn, Louis. II. Title.
NA6813.U62N487   1997
727.7'09746'809 — DC21   97-5923
CIP

A catalogue record for this book
is available from the British Library.

The paper in this book meets the guidelines
for permanence and durability of the
Committee on Production Guidelines for Book Longevity
of the Council on Library Resources.

10   9   8   7   6   5   4   3   2   1

I sense Light as the giver of all presences,
and material as spent Light. What is made by Light
casts a shadow, and the shadow belongs to Light.
I sense a Threshold: Light to Silence, Silence to Light —
an ambiance of inspiration, in which the desire to be,
to express, crosses with the possible.

Louis I. Kahn

View from the northwest

I The Yale Center for British Art was founded in 1966 when Paul Mellon, Yale College class of 1929, announced his intention to give his unparalleled collection of British art to his alma mater, together with funds to build and endow an appropriate permanent home. He explained his reasons, and his expectations for the Center, in words which cannot be improved upon as a statement of purpose for the institution he created:

> *Since a university is a community of scholars, a majority of them young scholars at that, and since within its walls there is, or at least should be, a sharing of interests and a cross-fertilization of knowledge, it seemed to me that the ferment of a university would enliven and stimulate the study of and the enjoyment of these artistic relics of our British inheritance, more vitally and more resourcefully than if they were passively displayed in a non-teaching institution.*

The Center opened on April 15, 1977. Among its inaugural publications was *The Architecture of the Yale Center for British Art* by Jules David Prown, director from 1968 to 1976, which chronicled the genesis of the building. Twenty years later we return to the subject thanks to the initiative of the internationally renowned photographer David Finn, who has roamed the structure with his camera to record it not in plan or principle, but in glass, steel, and concrete fact—a successful, living building which matures with every year of useful activity.

We should begin, however, by revisiting the days of creation, of the fruitful collaboration between client and architect which Jules Prown has described from his perspective as the former of the two. In January 1969, before the architect was chosen, he laid out the ground rules:

The architecture ... should be consistent with the collection of British art that is the heart of the Center. British art is extraordinarily reflective of the society that produced it, suffused with those values that have characterized life in England and in those societies that Englishmen have helped to establish throughout the world. It is an art of places, and human activities. It relates to the real world and what goes on there. The Center must be informed by a similar concern with people and with life. Rather than a pure abstract statement of architectural form, its building must relate to the people who will use it. In a word, the building must be humanistic.

From the start the building was conceived of contextually:

The arts at Yale are concentrated in the vicinity.... Commercially, an increasing number of fine apparel stores, specialty gift shops, book stores, restaurants, and other pleasurable enterprises are clustered [there]. There is an obvious and important opportunity at hand to contribute substantially through the design of the Center to making this area of Yale and New Haven humane, delight-filled and life-enhancing.

Several months later, in the autumn of 1969, the University announced the appointment of Louis I. Kahn as the architect. Jules Prown wrote at the time: "Louis Kahn is, in my opinion, the greatest American architect of our time, uniquely equipped to respond to the opportunity afforded Yale and New Haven by Paul Mellon's gift. He is a remarkable human being, sensitive both to the inner world of art and the external world of everyday existence." Among his highest qualifications counted "a highly developed urban sense, honed by considerable experience in urban planning. In the present instance, he is intimately familiar with the

2

Chapel Street shops

site for the Center, located directly across the street from the Art Gallery he built over fifteen years ago and ... where he taught."

In 1969 neither Kahn nor Prown could have envisaged the building we inhabit today. There were all too many proverbial slips between the promised cup and the lips which drank congratulatory toasts in 1977. The most tragic of the unforeseen circumstances was the death of the architect in 1974, of the man who believed not in invention but in discovery, for whom a building, once realized, was a material and existential fact, projected forward into space and time. He returned to New Haven with an extraordinary list of achievements: the Salk Institute for Biological Studies in La Jolla, California, and the First Unitarian Church and School in Rochester, New York, which were finished buildings; Sher-e-Bangla Nagar,

3

Portico of central wing, Kimbell Art Museum
Fort Worth, Texas. Louis I. Kahn, architect

Pazzi Chapel, Santa Croce, Florence
Filippo Brunelleschi, architect

capital of Bangladesh, the Library at the Phillips Exeter Academy, and the Kimbell Art Museum in Fort Worth, Texas, which were all under construction. Each one is unique in form and specific as to function. They all bear some genetic relationship to the Center, although the Kimbell, as an art museum in progress, invites the closest comparison. There Kahn was in the process of realizing one of the most serene of all architectural statements, a long, low series of barrel-vaulted galleries of almost monastic purity. Vincent Scully and others have written at length about Kahn's debt to classical antiquity, from Paestum to Piranesi. Yet, for me, standing beside the grove of miniature holly trees which lines the forecourt of the Kimbell, it is Brunelleschi who comes to mind, above all the Brunelleschi of the Pazzi Chapel at Santa Croce in Florence.

4

Unsupported as the comparison may be from Kahn's own statements, it is hard to resist in terms of the clearly defined structure —defined, that is, by means of shallow curves and straight lines in regular and rhythmic interplay. It is friendly in scale, a glistening embodiment of human geometry. Admittedly the Kimbell uses smooth, gray concrete, instead of pietra serena, to enclose panels of travertine, not stucco, but it stands in Texas, in the late twentieth century, as an eloquent restatement of those principles of architectural humanism which we associate with the early Italian Renaissance.

In countless details the Center resembles its immediate predecessor. Yet, for all their similarities the differences between the two buildings are fundamental. In Fort Worth Kahn had come to terms with a totally different set of constraints as well as opportunities. Its nine-and-a-half acre site lies within a park shared by two other museums. Above it, on higher ground to the west, stands Philip Johnson's Amon Carter Museum of 1959, with a view over the city which the Kimbell's trustees agreed not to obstruct. On the other hand, the setting placed no restriction on horizontal development. In New Haven, by contrast, Kahn was given a densely built urban site with obligations to its civic and commercial past as well as to the adjacent buildings with which it was to share certain academic functions as an integral part of the University.

Believing as he did in discovery, one of Kahn's first instincts was to find out about British art in general and about the Paul Mellon Collection in particular. Jules Prown has described their visits together to New York, Virginia, and Washington, D.C., to see many of the works of art destined for the Center and to assess the future needs of the collection. To the press in Fort Worth Kahn had described his plan for the Kimbell as "a friendly home." As he got

Hardwick Hall, Derbyshire
The gallery as depicted in 1835

to know the Paul Mellon Collection, he responded with particular
warmth to the intimate scale and informal nature of many of the
paintings. From there he went on to consider the buildings in which
they were originally housed. English town and country houses are
often impressive but rarely overwhelming. From the sixteenth
century onward, coincidental with the rise of secular easel painting,
the emphasis in domestic architecture was increasingly upon
comfort as opposed to security. Improvements in the manufacture
of glass allowed windows to become larger, while abundant
supplies of wood and coal encouraged the generous deployment of
fireplaces. Both were prominent architectural features of the Long
Galleries which provided recreational space year-round to the
inhabitants of country houses. Gradually usage changed, as these

6

areas for indoor exercise were fitted and furnished with precious objects; by 1591 the word *gallery* had acquired a new meaning in the English language, denoting "an apartment or building for the display of works of art." Centuries later, Kahn embraced it in both senses, recognizing Long Galleries not only as precursors but as models, with their long ambulatory spaces and natural light, for the kind of architectural experiences he wished to provide in his galleries for British art. In conversation with his client he referred frequently to fireplaces as another feature with an important social function, providing focal points within the building for people to gather around in conversation. In virtually all of his sketches figures appear, standing, seated, gesticulating even when they are indicated by one or two summary strokes of the pencil, but never isolated or indifferent either to their surroundings or to one another.

If Jules Prown's account of the building has a fault, it lies in the underestimate of the part he played as the client, working directly on behalf of the University with both the architect and the donor. Fortunately he has written elsewhere of that role, one for which the daily users of the building have ample reason to be grateful. For architecture is not an abstract art; too often architects are blamed for the shortcomings of clients who fail to brief them properly. Not only did Jules Prown help to articulate the underlying principles of the Center, setting those priorities which guided the University toward the inspired choice of Louis Kahn; he also went on to detail a program of future use which the architect could embody in built form. Kahn liked to speak in anatomical terms, referring to the mechanical rooms as lungs and the air shafts through which they were ventilated as nostrils. He could do so effectively in part because his client's careful assessment of practical requirements

Air shaft

allowed him to think of the building organically, as growing out of clearly stated needs and carefully defined functions.

Between conception and execution a good many practical considerations intervened. They emerge, when one reads between the lines of the minutes and memoranda of meetings held during construction, as different codes and regulations threatened to compromise the integrity of Kahn's architectural vision. Above all, there was the problem of escalating costs. Parts of the building were scaled down, and contingencies were drawn up to substitute less expensive materials. Some of the losses were serious, to the shipping and receiving areas of the building, for instance, but in other cases the discipline of revision led to improvements in the design. The Center as built is far more compact in plan and elevations than the earlier projects. By all accounts Kahn responded philosophically and practically to these austerity measures, insisting only on truth to materials. Cement blocks could be substituted for poured concrete, for example, as long as the replacement was undisguised.

8

Throughout the process he clung to his initial, bifocal conception, two halves of a single building which reflected the dual nature of the Center itself. At different times in the design process the bifurcation was differently expressed in architectural terms. But the basic concept remained: the building is organized around two interior courts; the first, at the entrance, gives unimpeded access, especially to the three floors of galleries above; the second, a floor higher, is more secluded and leads to the Reference Library, the Print Room, and the Rare Book Room. Yet, in identifying the two courtyards with the twinned purposes of the Center as a public museum and a research institute, it is important to remember that they are organically and structurally linked, like the two wings of the lepidopteral analogy Kahn drew in answer to the question: how will the building look? "On a grey day it will look like a moth; on a sunny day, like a butterfly."

View from the northeast

2 Other figures of speech come to mind, but Kahn's prediction of changing appearances proved uncannily accurate. On a dull day the burnished steel panels are soft and light-absorbent, like bales of good gray English cloth. The building is solemn. In bright light the windows in the façades shine with reflections; they serve as mirrors held to the sky, the trees, and the buildings opposite. It smiles. Kahn's affection for Egerton Swartwout's Sculpture Hall is manifest in the views of it he provided from most of the rooms on the north side of the Center and even more so in the care he took to capture its reflections in his own façade, as if to associate the ghostly shades of the Italian Renaissance with his own innovative yet deeply respectful architecture.

The building also changes according to our angle of vision. It can be impressive and imposing, as when it is seen from across the street at the intersection of Chapel and High Streets; a gigantic steel case, girded with bands of concrete, its freestanding column at the cutaway corner entrance giving the impression that it is raised on stilts above the bustling activity of the street. (In a sense it is: like the great Renaissance libraries by Michelangelo and Wren, Kahn's building protects its treasures by elevating them above the marshy thoroughfare beneath, in light and airy, user-friendly space.) Alternatively, if you approach from the south, along High Street, past the Cambridge Arms and the other four- and five-story apartment buildings in a variety of undistinguished architectural styles, the Center closes ranks in a tactful, unassuming way. It does so by respecting the scale and proportions of its neighbors, in spite of its own running footage of more than one hundred and twenty feet. It insists on not obtruding, preferring to reiterate the vertical accents of the adjacent townhouses with its own far more ordered bay divisions. Between these apartments, with their impoverished

South façade

echoes of collegiate gothic, and the Yale campus, with its cacoph-
ony of architectural revivals, the Center stands in exemplary, but
by no means reproachful, silence.

Silence is perhaps the wrong word, although one commentator,
David Brownlee, has described the building as a "mute prism."
I prefer to retain Kahn's cherished illusion of a "fusion of the
senses" in which "space has tonality and I imagine myself
composing a space lofty, vaulted, or under a dome, attributing to
it a sound character alternating with the tones of the space, narrow
and high, with graduating silver, light to darkness." His buildings
begin as themes, upon which he composes and displays an infinitely
subtle series of variations.

Southeast corner

At first sight the Center's rectangular façades appear to be lego-like: uniform panels of steel and glass attached on all four sides to the reinforced concrete framework of the building. Closer inspection reveals the painstaking refinement of architectural expression. For example, on three of the façades, the horizontal lines drawn by the concrete beams disappear between the second and third floors, where the spaces behind them are double-storied. Outside and inside, the columns are thinned as they ascend toward the light-bearing roof, and thickened as they carry floor-by-floor weight downward toward the load-bearing foundations. The heavy concrete lintels which separate the first and second floors on the north and south sides have a similar structural logic; along Chapel Street they also make a firm distinction between the Center above and the shops beneath.

13

The early decision on the part of the University to incorporate shops into the street frontage of the building may have been expedient, but it was equally inspired. Had the Center not included them, it would have broken the fragile ribbon of commercial development which threads its way westward from New Haven's historic Green to Upper Chapel Street, where local stores and small restaurants lead the campaign for urban renewal. Kahn obviously welcomed the challenge of fitting his building into the urban context. High Street and York Street are partly residential and partly commercial. The north side of Chapel Street is part of the Yale campus, while the south side belongs to the city of New Haven. The Center unites all of these elements in yet another "friendly home" for that life-enhancing, communal property called art.

One of Kahn's earliest sketches shows a succession of small shops built into an arcade facing Chapel Street. It is inscribed "Palazzo Melloni," a wonderfully apt designation which on the one hand reveals the architectural source for his thoughts and on the other draws a telling parallel between his patron and those Renaissance princes, like the Medici, who built palaces to house their incomparable art collections but were sufficiently canny to provide within them, at street level, rentable commercial space.

For the pedestrian on Chapel Street, it is the shops which animate the building, especially as the light fades and their illuminated windows draw eyes inward, encouraging the passersby to enter beneath those massy lintels to experience the pleasures of consumption: food, wine, books, clothes, and jewelry. In contrast, there is something reticent about the Center's entrance: austere by comparison, obligingly and appropriately negative in relation to its commercial neighbors. But, above all, accessible: bluestone sills and

Shops

brick paving lead quietly beneath the corner canopy, an extension of the sidewalk into the Entrance Court.

Before we enter, a final observation. For many visitors the outside of the building remains, at best, aloof. I have tried to explain its subtlety and its civic virtue, but I cannot help feeling that there is something deliberate about its understatement. Thanks to David Finn's photographs, we can dwell upon its every detail, in which concrete and steel are joined and glass reflects to create an architectural integrity which has been achieved all too rarely in the western tradition since Greek colonists raised the temples of Paestum on the Italian peninsula. Yet, it offers few clues to what it contains. Only those reflections in the windows, modern quotations from the stones of Venice and Florence, of Peter Wight

15

and Egerton Swartwout, indebted in equal proportions to John Ruskin, hint at "The Art of England" which lies within. I suspect that the dramatist in Kahn (a quality common to great architects and composers) relished the contrast between the reticence of the Center's outside walls, with their uncompromising refusal to recede from the exterior surfaces of the building, and the interior spaces in which steel concedes to wood, stone to woolen carpet. Spaces and textures alike are softened into seemingly endless vistas of visual pleasure. Shades of darkness are replaced by shades of light.

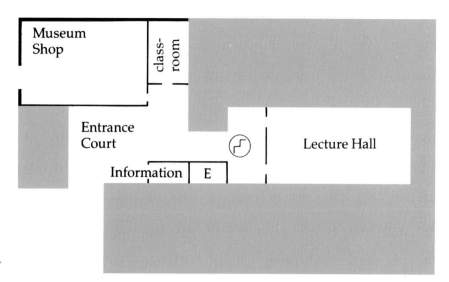

First floor

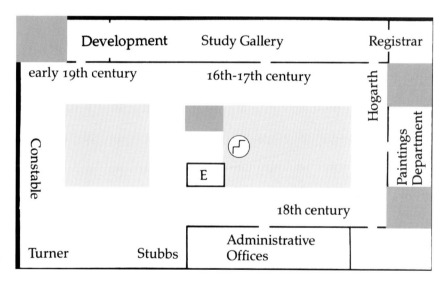

Fourth floor

Entrance Court

3

The portico is a generous space by any standard. Some forty feet square and eleven feet high, two of its sides are open to Chapel and High Streets, respectively. The absence of columns from both façades lends dramatic emphasis to its width and depth. Under foot the grid of the building is traced out by strips of bluestone which divide the brick paving into four equal squares. Overhead it is restated by the troughs of lighting canisters which hang like hollow beams from the smoothly formed, poured gray concrete ceiling. Above and below, this linear pattern appears to be tied to the one central freestanding column, the only load-bearing vertical element placed as a solitary pier between the sidewalk and the entrance to the Center.

An irresistible logic informed Kahn's decision to open the northeast corner of the building as the entrance to the Center. In no other place did he allow anything to interrupt the smooth planes and unbroken surfaces of his façades. An attached portico would have been as unthinkable as any other projection beyond the pristine geometry of the prism, leaving recession as the only alternative form of emphasis. The result is an appropriation of interior space, to provide a sheltering transition between the street outside and the courtyard inside. The steel panels are bent inward in elegant curves, away from the concrete columns. The weather-resistant materials of the exterior carry through into the heart of the building. Even with the lights on, the portico is never brightly lit. It offers shade, cover, but not enclosure to the visitor, who is drawn through it by the unrevealed source of light beyond the glass doors of the entrance itself. Once over the threshold, the mystery is solved. Interior space soars upward, through all four stories of the building toward the natural source of illumination.

Portico

Isabella Stewart Gardner Museum

On three sides the first floor of the Entrance Court is lined in steel. Set between gray concrete columns, it restates the cool metallic reticence of the exterior in counterpoint to the white-oak paneling to which it gives way, on all four sides, around the three floors above. There is a similarly gentle but insistent transition between the dark floor bricks and bluestone outside under the portico and the pale travertine marble paving the entrance courtyard inside. Shafts of sunlight play on honey-colored paneled walls, which are pierced here and there on the upper floors to offer glimpses of the exhibition spaces beyond. All at once the building seems to open up around us, and we are reminded how fruitful the Mediterranean courtyard plan has proved to be, not only here but as a source of museum architecture in this country for well over a century: the Isabella Stewart Gardner Museum in Boston and the Fogg Art

Museum in Cambridge, Massachusetts, for instance, or the Walters Art Gallery in Baltimore and the Frick Collection in New York. Kahn's references are indirect, befitting a culture which has basked, whenever possible, in Mediterranean sunshine. But unlike the patrician marble halls which eighteenth-century Englishmen designed for exclusive use, the Entrance Court of the Center enjoys a democratic relationship to the street. To judge from Kahn's early designs, he was tempted to leave it open to the sky (a solution more attuned to the climate of Texas than Connecticut), but even when he roofed it over, he managed to retain something of that sense of a small paved cortile dotted with trees and wooden benches, into which the noise and bustle of the streets beyond penetrates as a distant murmur.

Like the portico, the Entrance Court appropriates 1,600 square feet, another four of the twenty-foot squares on the plan of the building. That stated, the rest is contrast: between the low ceiling and the high roof, between shade and sunlight, as our eyes are drawn irresistibly upward through all four floors to the cluster of four vaults, each glazed with four shallow pods or domes. Once again, the geometry of the building is clearly stated, and its modular structure is articulated with the same precision and refinement observed outside; from the second floor upward the concrete columns are thinned and further recessed between the oak panels as they carry less and less weight, floor by floor, up to the roof. The careful detailing of the paneling itself sets the style and the standard for millwork throughout the building; the rectangular panels are flush with their frames, separated only by means of vertical and horizontal grooves between the two elements. The finish is that of cabinetmaking rather than carpentry—of an exquisitely designed piece of furniture in which hardware alone, hinges and handles, indicates the presence of doors such as those

Glazed domes

into the seminar room. Access from the Entrance Court to the museum shop was an afterthought, designed in 1985 by Kahn's associate, Marshall Meyers, when the Center took over one of the commercial spaces for its own use. Inevitably, there was a sacrifice: the doorway replaces a coat closet which once balanced on the left the closet still to the right of the classroom doors.

Leaving the courtyard involves another dramatic architectural contrast related directly to entering it from the street. To the west another forty-foot lintel lowers the concrete ceiling down to a single story, its thickness exposed to stress its load above and the horizontal void beneath. In Kahn's original design, in which the courtyard was open alike to the sky and the street, the formal entrance to the Center would have been at this point. Figuratively,

23

Threshold to the interiors

it remains so: a final threshold to the interiors. Straight ahead are the stairs, encased in their freestanding concrete cylinder. Beyond lies the lecture hall, a two-hundred-seat auditorium raking steeply down to basement level, a carpeted and upholstered concrete box with excellent acoustics and uninterrupted sight lines for every member of its audience. And to left and right, as alternatives to the stairs, freight and passenger elevators, their matte-steel doors set into the twinned concrete service towers which mark the center of the building.

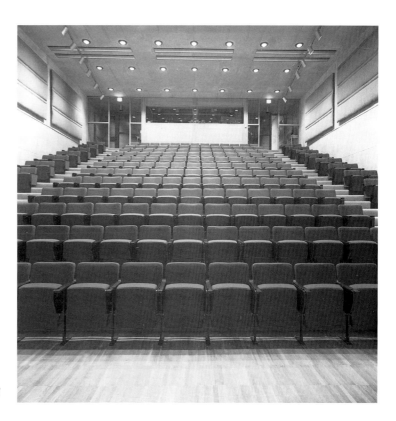

Lecture Hall

View from the northwest

High Street from the south

High Street façade

Portico

Entrance Court

Entrance Court

Entrance Court

Glazed domes

Entrance Court

Lecture Hall

Lecture Hall

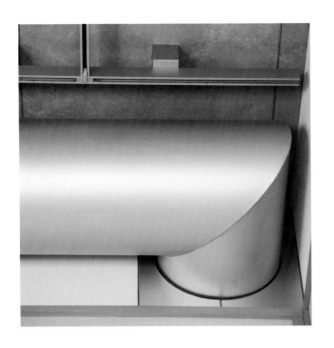

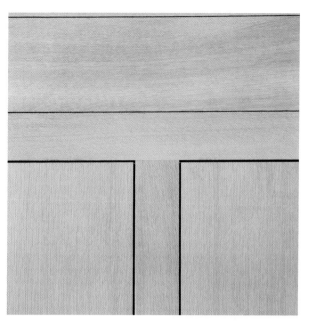

Turner bay

Fourth-floor galleries

Fourth-floor galleries

Third-floor galleries

Library Court

Library Court

Reference Library

Print Room

Fourth-floor galleries

4

The choices which confront the visitor are as varied as the contents of the Center, with its collections, classrooms, offices, and study rooms. But the newcomer is well advised to begin on the fourth floor, the *piano nobile* of sky-lit picture galleries covering more than 20,000 square feet of interconnected public space. As you emerge from the elevator on the fourth floor and turn left, you look into and across the upper paneled walls of the entrance court. Before you begin to tour the galleries, the building assures you of orientation; you can always see ahead and look back; there are no culs-de-sac or blind corners. Carpet under foot adds a further level of comfort to the light-filled spaces in which the permanent collection of paintings hangs. The travertine reappears briefly on this and the two floors beneath it, in the foyer-like areas between the elevator towers. It is then confined to narrow strips which articulate the grid of the building around each of the twenty-foot squares and provide firm supports for the movable panels that create the succession of room-like spaces. All nonstructural interior walls are covered with unbleached linen, complementing the warm tone of the other furnishings, the undyed woolen carpets, and the trim of untreated white oak. All these surfaces absorb the light— that filtered and directed daylight which on the fourth floor floods down from baffled skylights to be softened by the smooth gray concrete coffers of the ceiling and then distributed evenly onto the picture-bearing surfaces of the gallery's walls. Daylight is the key to the success of the fourth floor. It is also admitted sideways through the windows that afford a view out onto the campus on the north side and across the rooftops of New Haven to the east and south. This acknowledgment of the world outside ranks highly among those humane features which Prown called for and Kahn supplied; it is fundamental to the experience of pleasure within the building.

William Hogarth (1697–1764)
"The Beggar's Opera," III, xi, 1729
oil on canvas

Daylight in the context of European easel painting is natural in
more senses than one. Artists worked by it and their patrons took
it for granted. Occasionally they installed skylights in studios and
picture galleries, but most of the time they relied in their houses
upon conventional windows for illumination by day. There is
plenty of visual evidence, including paintings of interiors. Turner,
for instance, made a watercolor of the drawing room at Farnley
Hall in Yorkshire, where his patron Walter Fawkes lived. It is a
view looking down the room toward the end wall, where his own
painting of *The Dort Packet-Boat from Rotterdam Becalmed*
occupied pride of place above the fireplace, taking full advantage
of the light which streamed through the windows along the wall to
the left. It is safe to state that both Turner and Fawkes appreciated
the importance of placing the canvas in a position which would
allow it to glow in side light, reinforcing the hidden source of

28

sunlight in the painting itself, glistening where it falls and casting shadows to the right. Here in the Center that same painting enjoys the identical compliment, thanks to its position on an east wall with a window at right angles admitting the best of all, north light. Standing back within the room, which contains a dozen or so of Turner's most important oils and measures twenty by forty feet, you suddenly realize that for all the difference in style, Kahn's rooms are faithful to the domestic scale of eighteenth- and nineteenth-century British architecture. They are impressive without being palatial; they are well matched to the objects they were designed to display.

The Paul Mellon Collection is rich in sporting paintings, conversation pieces, interiors, and landscapes with figures—all of them intimate and, by comparison with the great life-sized icons of British portraiture, informal in their treatment of their respective subjects. Scenes like Hogarth's, from John Gay's *Beggar's Opera*, or portraits like Reynolds's of Mrs. Abington in her celebrated role as Miss Prue in Congreve's *Love for Love* are masterpieces of painting. They are important, among other reasons, for the light they shed on eighteenth-century theatrical conventions but above all because they introduce new standards of social commentary and psychological insight into the art of the period. To appreciate them fully requires close attention to painted detail: the double-entendre of Polly Peachum's imploring gaze which the actress Lavinia Fenton skillfully redirects off-stage, toward her real-life admirer, the Duke of Bolton; Mrs. Abington's clever mastery of her part as a somewhat younger and much less intelligent woman; such subtleties can only be relished in the nearest equivalent to armchair comfort a picture gallery can supply.

29

Window shutters

From his sketches onward Kahn planned for an intimate relationship between objects and their viewers. He also appreciated the need to relax between bouts of visual concentration. At regular intervals the visitor is offered vistas, through the windows, or across and down into the atrium. The addition in 1981 of the wooden window shutters Kahn had envisaged originally added significantly to the furnishing of the building. It did so without any modification to the structure; the rigid panels glide in and out of the wall cavities within the existing window frames. The design of the shutters themselves is entirely traditional. They are an indoor variant in white oak of those hinged shutters which migrated westward from the Mediterranean and remain popular in domestic architecture today, two centuries later, as a form of exterior decoration, although they have lost their utility in the air-conditioned twentieth century. Kahn's remain strictly functional. By the simplest manual operation, they adjust to admit or block daylight to varying degrees. Like glazing bars, they give definition to the window plane and the separation of interior from exterior

30

Window onto Chapel Street

space. They confirm the position of the viewer as they frame and furnish the views they disclose, of the Ghibelline crenellations on top of Swartwout's tower to the north, or the flat, asphalt rooftops punctuated by vent pipes and air-conditioning units, an urban landscape worthy of Richard Estes, to the east.

Inside the building Kahn's architectural details quietly complement the paintings on the walls. The elegant proportions of eighteenth-century London outlined in exquisite detail by Canaletto's brush are echoed in Kahn's manipulation of built forms. Take the fine lines he has drawn between steel and concrete, where elements meet in and around the service columns, for instance, which the

31

Canaletto (1697–1768)
St. Paul's Cathedral, 1754
oil on canvas

V-shaped roof beams convert into graceful spires of gray metal. The roof beams themselves meet one another without fusion, each retaining its pre-cast integrity as a building block, fitting exactly into place within the rhythmic geometry of the whole. Different materials never invade one another, even when they meet on the same plane. Strips of oak frame the linen panels on the walls, screens rise to within a few inches of the beams or ceilings to which they are tied, and they stand free of the concrete columns on either side. The circulation of light and air throughout the building brings to mind again Kahn's belief in its organic life, a belief he shared with the seventeenth-century architect of those painted views of London, Christopher Wren.

A great deal of thought has gone into the positioning of screens throughout the galleries. As a result the fourth floor offers a variety

32

Fourth-floor galleries

of spaces, from the long vistas and diagonal sight lines which show to best advantage those full-length patricians painted by van Dyck in the seventeenth century, by Lawrence in the nineteenth, and by Reynolds and Gainsborough in between, to far more intimate enclosures, near to the windows, created to display oil sketches that are small in scale, such as Constable's sky studies. Once again daylight is essential to a full appreciation; daylight in all its variable intensity is fundamental to the naturalism of nineteenth-century landscape painters whose canvases are all too easily flattened by even beams of artificial light. Happily the Center allows for far greater flexibility with respect to space and light than contemporary museum practice favors. Kahn's building will adjust, effortlessly, to future curatorial priorities.

33

Study Gallery

To judge from his drawings, Kahn favored unbroken corridors
of display space, reminiscent of the Long Galleries he admired
in English manor houses. The south side of the fourth floor is
so arranged to provide an open reserve, or Study Gallery, for
paintings. It runs through seven consecutive bays to which glass-
walled offices at both ends add a further forty feet, bringing the
linear total to one hundred and eighty feet. Parallel screens placed
at right angles to the wall opposite the windows create bays in
which some four hundred paintings hang, stacked from floor
to ceiling for the practical purpose of making as much of the
collection accessible as possible under the same daylit conditions as
the main galleries. The effect resembles a nineteenth-century picture
gallery such as that of Lord Northwick at Thirlestaine House,

34

Robert Huskisson (fl. 1832–1854)
*Lord Northwick's Picture Gallery
at Thirlestaine House*, c. 1846–47
oil on canvas

which we know from the painting by Robert Huskisson in the collection. Whether they make the connection or not, many visitors enjoy the contrast between the primary galleries, where the emphasis is upon eye-level viewing of carefully selected images, and the crowded intimacy of the Study Gallery, with its apparent freedom from curatorial determinations. What was designed to satisfy the needs of scholars all too accustomed to the frustration of gaining access to, let alone seeing, works of art in storage has become one of the most popular features of the Center.

Oak doors punctuate the gallery walls at intervals, and sections of paneling indicate the existence of service areas behind: restrooms, fire exits, and the like. The only signs are those required for safety reasons, ensuring that the only labels are those relative to the works of art on display. I have often been asked why offices, including the director's, are not identified as such. My explanation is that they must be seen as secondary to the galleries which

35

Director's Office   *Business Office*

surround them, to those dedicated spaces in which nothing is allowed to detract from the visual experience of art and architecture. In one respect, however, the offices do serve as extensions of the galleries. The reserves of paintings are arranged throughout them, including the business office, in which scenes of chivalric combat vie for attention with representations of rage, grief, and despair, thanks to the large number of eighteenth-century history paintings hanging there.

No visitor leaves the fourth floor unaware of the plan of the entire building. Pausing to look down into either of the two courtyards, we absorb its symmetry, recognizing the familiar landscape of the Entrance Court and encountering not once but several times the far more furnished and enclosed space of the Library Court, the view from above dominated by its upholstered seating and brightly colored oriental carpet. The invitation is irresistible.

36

View into Library Court

View into Entrance Court

Second-floor galleries

5

When the Center first opened, the display of the permanent collection of paintings was confined to the fourth floor. At that stage the chronological boundaries of the collections were defined by three centuries; and although there was every expectation of future growth, with few exceptions works were acquired only if the artist was born before 1850. The subsequent decision, which the founder endorsed, to relax that restriction has encouraged expansion well into the nineteenth and twentieth centuries. By 1984 it was clear that the permanent collection, which gave rise to the building in the first place, deserved a greater proportion of the available space. Originally both the second- and third-floor galleries had been designated for temporary exhibitions. Of these, only the third floor, from which daylight is excluded on three sides, is ideal for the display of works on paper and other light-sensitive materials. The second-floor galleries, on the other hand, are well

Third-floor galleries

39

endowed with windows in the exterior walls and openings in the paneling around the Entrance Court. The logic of the architecture made the curatorial choice inevitable. For the past ten years the third floor has been dedicated to temporary exhibitions in all media. The fourth-floor galleries display paintings and sculpture before about 1820, and the second floor is devoted to art since then.

In deference to Victorian taste, the paintings of the mid-nineteenth century are tightly packed into a series of smaller rooms created with screens of different widths, some of them deliberately blocking the horizontal flow of daylight from the windows in favor of artificial light from incandescent lamps. The flat concrete ceiling from which the cylindrical air ducts are suspended add the faintest touch of claustrophobia. The effect is contrived; eventually it is dispelled as the figurative cobwebs are blown away by the access to more daylight, befitting the breezy naturalism adopted by the members of the New English Art Club and the Glasgow Boys.

View across Entrance Court

The views from the second-floor galleries down into the Entrance Court are among the most satisfying within the building. Closer to ground level and to the tops of the trees in the courtyard, the openings seem more intimate than those under the lofty vaults above the fourth floor. Height bestows privilege; you can look down from the second floor, almost within reach of everything below, and remain unobserved in the shadows of your own balcony. These are natural vantage points from which to see the building in different lighting and perspective. Here the proximity to works of art of the twentieth century may serve to heighten awareness of abstract patterns in the fabric itself: in the steel squares, the oak panels, and the smooth concrete columns to which they are so respectfully attached. Abstract yet irresistibly tactile:

in places where the concrete is exposed to the touch of human hands, the gradual process of patination which began in the forms into which the cement was poured has continued, enriching the surfaces with the record of past encounters, further evidence of the life within the building. Accidental beauty has been a tenet of artistic faith at least since the Renaissance; and while Kahn believed fervently that "to make a thing deliberately beautiful is a dastardly act," David Finn captures in plate after plate the unselfconscious beauty of the architecture.

Of all the elements in the building, the concrete cylinder encasing the stairs is by far the most assertive. Standing in the basement, with the elevators to the left and the right, the whole environment is one of weight and mass, consisting almost entirely of gray steel and gray concrete, with the staircase rising like a mighty fortress, cutting through the floors above with the kind of insistent geometry Kahn applied to his buildings in Bangladesh and at the Phillips Exeter Academy. It also reflects upon his stairwell across the street, in his first public building, his extension of 1951–53 of the Yale University Art Gallery. Both are ingenious, three-dimensional exercises in the mathematical problem of accommodating the square to the circle. Only the slightly fussy treatment of guards and hand-rails in the case of the Center dilutes the drama of climbing up or down the hollow spiral, and they are, in all probability, the work of the successor architects following Kahn's death in 1974. On each floor the staircase establishes its formidable presence. In the Library Court it stands tall, as if detached from the floors to which it gives access, a round tower within the space which is, to all intents and purposes, the Center's baronial hall. Materially the drum echoes the concrete of the columns and the roof beams, but it remains sturdily independent, refusing to touch them, for

First-floor foyer   *Stairwell cylinder*

the perfectly good reason that structurally it has nothing to do with them.

The differences between the Center's two courtyards are salient and subtle. Both are essential to circulation, but the Entrance Court, in providing access to the entire building, is the more public space. To reach the Library Court involves going to the second floor. We leave as we enter, from the center of the building, and access from it is to places of study and contemplation. The Entrance Court is surrounded on all three floors above by picture galleries, while the Library Court admits visitors right and left to the Print Room and to the Reference Library, to the academic activities of the Center. In doing so it maintains the focus upon the collections in a space which is large enough to accommodate several hundred people and provides an ideal setting for chamber

43

Library Court

music. The oak-paneled walls are lined with full-length portraits dating from the late sixteenth to the early nineteenth centuries. Facing the entrance are two of George Stubbs's greatest canvases, his *Lion Attacking a Horse* and *Lion Attacking a Stag*. They fill the wall with their dramatic presentation of "nature red in tooth and claw," in counterpoint to the high fashions and social graces displayed all around them. Among the cool white marble busts which stand at eye level below, those two old political foes, Charles James Fox and William Pitt, stare in stony silence at one another from opposite sides of the room.

44

Library Court

Behind the three walls of the Library Court, study and storage
areas are arranged simply and effectively. During the design stages
there was considerable discussion about the relation of the
collection of rare books to the Reference Library of secondary
reading materials on the one hand and to the curatorial
Department of Prints and Drawings on the other. Kahn's solution
admits several organizational solutions, as the subsequent history
of the collections has demonstrated. The Print Room on the north
side and the Reference Library on the south are similar, two-story
spaces furnished differently in accordance with their respective
functions. From the public areas of the building their inter-
connection on the west is concealed by the short wall of the Library
Court, behind which the Rare Book Room, also double in height,

45

Rare Book Room

links the two and their respective offices. Circulation for staff and authorized users is maintained on both the second and the third floors, where long narrow galleries run the lengths of the study room beneath what are, in effect, clerestories admitting ambient daylight into the well-like spaces below. Careful detailing is everywhere. Cylindrical steel ducts carry the conditioned air at ceiling height on all but the fourth floor. In study areas their profile is echoed by the overhead light shades, suspended from tracks attached to, rather than channeled into, the poured concrete ceilings. Every form takes pride in its function. Each space is finely adjusted to its users' needs. I recall with lasting pleasure my first introduction to the Center as a visitor to the Print Room, when I sat day after day at the study tables placed at right angles to the

Print Room

Reference Library

windows, through which unfiltered north light ensured the best of all possible viewing conditions for box after box of English drawings. Similarly, in the Reference Library individual carrels are arranged in pairs, between the windows, separated by back-to-back bookshelves, all made from the same meticulously finished white oak. It is used to the point of lavishness in the paneled oak staircases which join the Print Room to the stacks above and the Reference Library to the balcony which houses the Photograph Archive. Almost as secretive as the hidden stairs to some manorial priest's hole, they are exquisitely crafted pieces of interior furniture, which repeat, on a miniature scale, that initial embrace of the Entrance Court, welcoming, reassuring, and whispering of hidden treasures. A private echo of the original, public statement.

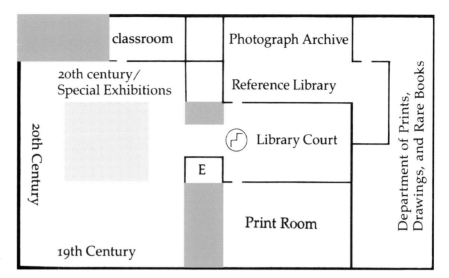

Second floor

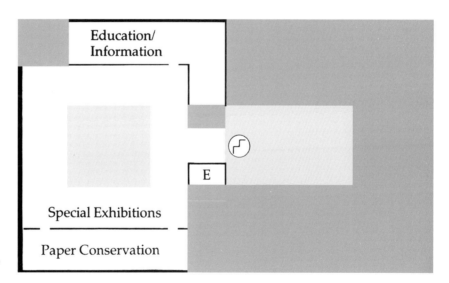

Third floor

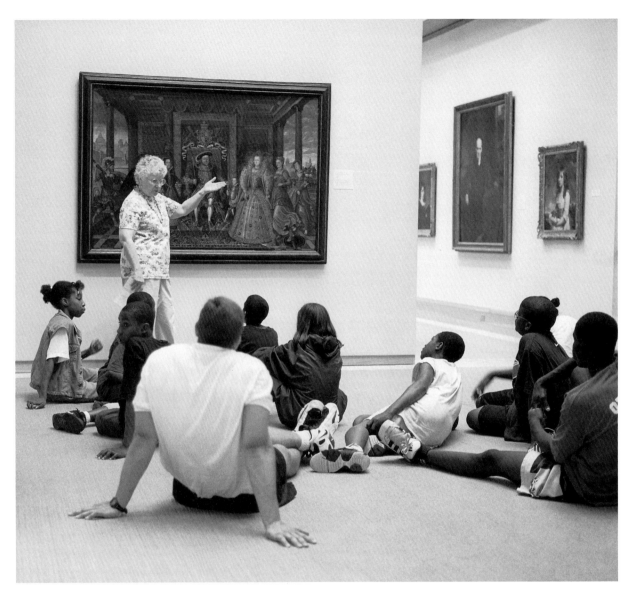

Docent with schoolchildren

6 Architectural historians will continue to debate Kahn's final building. For some it is conservative, while for others it marks a new threshold in a career which, for all its consistency, was full of surprises. Jules Prown, who knows better than anyone how many decisions were based on practical necessity, nonetheless speaks of the building's poetry, of its embodiment of those ethical values which he, as the client, did so much to articulate. Yet there are no contradictions here. We know from his art and architecture (or rather from his art in two and three dimensions) that Kahn relied heavily upon the past for inspiration. Among the sketches he made as a traveler in Europe and the Near East there are studies of pyramids and temples, Italian hill towns and medieval churches. All of his museum buildings disclose his instinctive grasp of the issues, of the museum as a combination of shrine, temple, and palace. And if Brunelleschi comes to mind in Fort Worth, Alberti takes his place in New Haven: the urban Alberti of the Palazzo Rucellai in Florence, with its delicate but severe geometry and its discreet classical allusions, conservative even as it introduced a renaissance in domestic architecture.

Although no one is more deserving than Kahn of the posthumous fame he enjoys, some of his more fervent admirers are prone to overlook the practical side of his nature. The building history of the Center reveals an architect of unusual flexibility who was prepared to go back to the drawing board to solve problems, whether they originated in cost, materials, or changes to the program. If anything, second thoughts seem to have concentrated his mind upon greater clarity of architectural expression. Throughout the process he was sustained by his belief, in Prown's words, "that a building is not simply a response to necessity." On the other hand, he never denied that it resulted from specific needs, in this case those identified first by the patron, who wished to find an

Palazzo Rucellai, Florence
Leon Battista Alberti, architect

appropriate institutional home for his collection with an appropriate building to house it, and then by the client, in receipt of his
princely gift. To interpret those and to fuse them successfully
required the kind of alchemy in which Kahn specialized. For, as we
have seen, there is a touch of the banker's palace in the four-square
block of the Center, hinting subliminally at that tradition which
originated in fifteenth-century Italy and in which, more immedi-
ately, Paul Mellon succeeded his father, the founder of the National
Gallery of Art in Washington, D.C. Far more consciously, the
building expressed the aspirations of its owner, a great research
university, rich in collections and increasingly aware of its
extramural responsibilities for education and intellectual welfare.
For the values embodied in this miraculous construction are not
those of the past. Although it accommodates handsomely the
collections in its care, it does not make the historical mistake of

52

Student visitors

trying to express their Zeitgeist. There is nothing preachy or revivalist here. The building is firmly in the present, dedicated to our belief in free access and enlightenment for all.

One of the greatest tributes the Center enjoys is the one paid constantly by the people who use it; it works. It works for the third-graders who visit it regularly as part of the City of New Haven's Comprehensive Arts Program; it works for high-school students from all over Connecticut, whose teachers actively incorporate material from the collections into their curricula; it works for undergraduates and graduate students not only of art history and not only at Yale; it works for advanced scholars from everywhere who are drawn by the collections to one of the most congenial of all research establishments. The litany continues;

53

lectures, concerts, plays, and performances of all kinds have been enjoyed in this setting, their successes now part of the intangible aura of a building which creative users have brought to life. Its heartbeat is human. Even the worn pile of the carpet speaks of appreciation, of pleasure sought and found in front of a favorite object, at a recital in the Library Court, or simply by strolling through the galleries in the company of friends, in cheerful acknowledgment of the arts as an essential part of civilized existence.

As the Yale Center for British Art celebrates its twentieth year, it is our privilege to look through the lens of David Finn's "third eye," the lens of his camera, at its architecture at work, fulfilling to the highest possible degree the ambitions and expectations of patron and client alike: "to enliven and to stimulate the study of and the enjoyment of the artistic relics" it enshrines. No more and no less than any great building, the Yale Center for British Art is a work of art in its own right.

Bibliography

Brown, Jack Perry. *Louis I. Kahn: A Bibliography*. New York: Garland, 1987.

Brownlee, David B., and David G. De Long. *Louis I. Kahn: In the Realm of Architecture*. New York: Rizzoli, 1991.

Crosbie, Michael J. "Evaluation: Monument Before Its Time." Yale Center for British Art, Louis Kahn. *Architecture* 75 (January 1986): 64–67.

Filler, Martin. "Opus Posthumous." *Progressive Architecture* 59, no. 5 (May 1978): 76–81.

Hubert, Bruno J. *Le Yale Center for British Art (Louis I. Kahn)*. Marseille: Editions Parenthèses, 1992.

Jordy, William. "Kahn at Yale." *Architectural Review* 162, no. 965 (July 1977): 37–44.

Loud, Patricia Cummings. *The Art Museums of Louis I. Kahn*. Durham, N.C.: Duke University Press, 1989.

Prown, Jules David. *The Architecture of the Yale Center for British Art*. New Haven, 1977; 2d ed., 1982.

_____. "On Being a Client." *Society of Architectural Historians Journal* 42, no. 1 (March 1983): 11–14.

Ronner, Heinz, and Sharad Jhaveri. *Louis I. Kahn: Complete Work, 1935–1974*. 2d ed. Basel: Birkhäuser Verlag, 1987.

Scully, Vincent J. "Yale Center for British Art." *Architectural Record* 161, no. 7 (June 1977): 95–104.